Original title:
Seeds of Soliloquy

Copyright © 2025 Creative Arts Management OÜ
All rights reserved.

Author: Clara Whitfield
ISBN HARDBACK: 978-1-80566-709-4
ISBN PAPERBACK: 978-1-80566-994-4

Layers of Untold Stories

In a world of tales untold,
Sprouts of humor subtly unfold.
A garden of giggles grows so bright,
Laughter blooms from day to night.

Whispers waltz on breezy days,
While squirrels plot their nutty ways.
Each leaf holds a secret grin,
Tickling thoughts from deep within.

A Solitary Roam in Thought

I wandered through my mind's own maze,
Tripping over forgotten phrase.
A rabbit hopped with quizzical eyes,
As I pondered life's silly ties.

Thoughts braiding in whimsical dance,
I slipped and fell in a trance.
The echoes of laughter rang so clear,
As silly daydreams drew me near.

The Garden of Mindful Wandering

In a garden where daydreams sprout,
Mice tell tales, casting doubt.
With each petal, a chuckle springs,
As butterflies plot their cheeky flings.

Tulips giggle in the sun,
Chatting about the silliest run.
Tickled by the breeze's play,
Where thoughts bloom in the light of day.

Tendrils of Thought Unfurled

Tendrils twist in playful jest,
My mind hosts its own comedy fest.
A sunflower winks, a daisy nods,
While ants debate the quirks of gods.

In this realm where chuckles reign,
I find joy in a little pain.
With every twist and every turn,
More lessons learned and laughter earned.

Moments of Quiet Discourse

In the silence, thoughts do sprout,
Whispered giggles, nodding about.
A squabble here, a chatter there,
Planted secrets in the air.

Footnotes drift like butterflies,
Pinching humor from the skies.
A nimble waltz, a silent dance,
Elusive wisdom, pure mischance.

Sown in Stillness: Unveiling Thoughts

A garden blooms in quiet pause,
Where laughter sprouts from silly flaws.
A gnarly thought, a twisty vine,
We chuckle 'til the sun does shine.

Beneath the surface, jokes reside,
Teasing whispers, hard to hide.
A playful poke, a jolly jest,
In stillness, minds find joy expressed.

The Lullaby of Thoughts

In soft repose, ideas play,
Bouncing like a child at play.
Tickling fancies with a grin,
Thoughts pirouette, let's begin!

A gentle nudge, a wink, a tease,
Laughter dances on the breeze.
A silly rhyme, a goofy tune,
In quiet moments, joy's in bloom.

Shadows of Reflection

Beneath the shade where quirks convene,
Lurking thoughts are rarely seen.
Cuckoo clocks with minds of their own,
Chime out laughter, seeds are sown.

In the quiet, echoes ring,
Tickled minds begin to sing.
A playful banter in the dark,
Witty shadows leave their mark.

Shards of Silence in the Wind

In the garden, whispers prance,
Cabbage dreams of a seaside dance.
Radishes sport their leafy hats,
While carrots chat with the chubby bats.

Chasing shadows, the sun does grin,
Telling tales of where it's been.
A dandelion blows, oh what a show,
Even the weeds hum a tune from below.

Fables of the Silent Seedbed

In the quiet, beans do boast,
Twisting tales from coast to coast.
Tomatoes giggle, red with glee,
As onions laugh in layers, you see.

Carrots sigh, oh what a plight!
Why do turnips flee from light?
Each tale unfolds with such flair,
In a patch of green, without a care.

Tides of Solitude and Reflection

The pond reflects a smiling frog,
Croaking verses in a log.
Dragonflies wear their finest suits,
While the goldfish brag about their roots.

Ripples ripple, giggles spread,
A turtle snores, dreams of bread.
In solitude, a dance is shared,
With every splash, the water's bared.

The Voice Beneath the Canopy

Under branches, whispers creep,
Where squirrels plan their next leap.
The owls hoot in riddles deep,
While the vines giggle, never sleep.

Mice exchange their late-night tales,
Plotting cheese heists, with tiny sails.
In this realm of leafy disguise,
Every rustle is a surprise.

Echoes of Silent Thoughts

Whispers bounce in empty air,
A squirrel stops to give a stare.
Thoughts collide, a bouncing ball,
With every giggle, I stand tall.

In my head, a circus plays,
Clowns on unicycles have their ways.
Juggling worries, one by one,
Until I trip and laugh, it's fun!

Inside my brain, a dance unfolds,
With funny hats and antics bold.
So take a seat, enjoy the show,
In this wild space, let laughter grow.

Threads of Introspection

Stitching thoughts like patchwork quilts,
My dreams are made of chocolate milks.
A needle pulls, it breaks, it slips,
And now I'm sewing with banana strips!

Twisted yarns of what I think,
Tangled songs that make me blink.
A yarn ball rolls, I chase it down,
Found a sock, and it's turned into a crown!

Every thread is quite a tale,
A cat's mischief never fails.
Wrap me up in giggles bright,
As I play with colors of sheer delight!

Fragments of a Quiet Mind

Puzzles in my quiet head,
Missing pieces, all misled.
Grouchy gnomes and dancing mice,
They argue over who's more nice.

Fragmented thoughts, a jigsaw mess,
I say "Aha!" as I dress.
I wear my socks in rainbow hues,
And trip on dreams that always amuse.

Minds can wander, minds can play,
Like cats that nap the day away.
In silence thunder roars aloud,
As I chuckle, quite proud!

Musings Beneath the Surface

Under waters deep and wide,
A fish is doing a silly slide.
With flip-flops made of bubble gum,
He sings a tune that's quite the hum!

Bubbles pop with silly sounds,
As turtles play on wobbly grounds.
Debating who can do the best,
A jiggle dance, a fishy fest!

Oceans full of giggle waves,
Splashing tales of silly braves.
Underneath, where laughter brews,
I float along, wearing my shoes!

The Tapestry of Inner Reflections

In the mirror of my mind, I see,
A jester dancing, wild and free.
With every thought, a silly prank,
Like ducks in bow ties on a plank.

Waves of nonsense crash and sway,
Tickling time in a goofy ballet.
The tapestry weaves, thread by thread,
As laughs balloon and worries shed.

My worries wear mismatched shoes,
As inner chatter sings the blues.
A carnival rides on this old brain,
Spinning round like a... well, insane!

So let the clowns paint my day bright,
With feathers and jokes, pure delight.
In this madcap, joyous quest,
The humor shines, I must confess.

Threefold Murmurs of Self

Whispers echo in a comical way,
Mind saying things that it shouldn't say.
A trio of me, just having a spree,
One's on a pogo stick, wild as can be.

In the garden of thought, giggles bloom,
We chase butterflies, light up the room.
Each murmur a riddle, wrapped in delight,
While my brain plays hopscotch, day turns to night.

A mime trapped in confusion's strong grip,
Spilling my secrets with a silly quip.
Threefold reflections, bouncing around,
Like rubber chickens that haven't been found.

So let's dance in this wacky parade,
Where laughter and nonsense aren't afraid.
Joyously fractured, we tumble and twirl,
In the merry madness, life's such a whirl.

The Labyrinth of Contemplative Tides

Lost in thought, I take a dip,
In a pool of giggles, a sassy slip.
Waves of wisdom, all out of sorts,
Sailing boats made of paper reports.

Each twist and turn, a punchline waits,
As I contemplate balancing plates.
Navigating nonsense, a whimsical glide,
In this maze of giggles, I take my stride.

Questions swirling like spaghetti strands,
Tangled ideas slip through my hands.
What's the answer? Who can tell?
As thoughts dive in to laugh and dwell.

In the mirthful tide, I find my flow,
Riding the currents where giggles grow.
Through the labyrinth, my laughter flies,
Out of chaos, clarity and pies.

Inner Landscapes of Solitary Thought

In my mind, a forest full of jest,
Trees wear hats and squirrels are dressed.
Thoughts tumble down like goofy leaves,
Chasing shadows that nobody believes.

A mountain of humor, I climb so high,
With clouds that tickle and stars that sigh.
Each peak a giggle, each valley a grin,
In the landscape of laughter, I dance and spin.

Fields of ponder, ripe with surprise,
Where every musing wears clownish ties.
Flowers of wit bloom wide and bright,
In this solitary play, all feels right.

So here in the woods of whimsy and glee,
I kick up the leaves and just let it be.
In the heart of my thoughts, a raucous cheer,
Gathering giggles year after year.

Tomes of Echoed Thoughts

In the library of my mind,
All the thoughts just laugh and bind.
Each page is filled with silly quips,
As I sip on air from cosmic sips.

Words tumble like a jester's dance,
As dialogues take a wild prance.
I argue with socks and ice cream,
In the whirlwind of this whimsical dream.

Constellations of Inner Dialogue

Stars in my head do twinkle bright,
Chasing whispers like a kite in flight.
I chat with cats about the moon,
And play hopscotch with thoughts in June.

Galaxies explode with giggles galore,
While burger buns sing – oh, encore!
Conversations with my couch ensue,
As it rolls its eyes, I'm born anew.

The Bloom of Private Thoughts

Beneath my hat, ideas sprout,
Dancing like a bug with a shout.
I pick a rose that talks in rhyme,
It tells me jokes about dinner time.

From underground came laughter's bloom,
Twirling around my cluttered room.
Thoughts in pots, so tongue-in-cheek,
Sprouting puns every single week.

Threads of Inner Serenity

In the loom of my quiet mind,
I stitch together threads, unwined.
With laughter woven into each seam,
My thoughts giggle like a bubbling stream.

Tangled yarns of goofy plots,
Whisper softly, tying knots.
Each twist and turn, a comedic flare,
Creating sweaters beyond compare.

The Unheard Symphony of Nature

In the garden where clovers play,
A frog croaks jokes to the bees each day.
The trees dance gently, their leaves in cheer,
While flowers giggle, spreading perfume near.

The sun winks bright, a mischievous spark,
As squirrels plot pranks from dawn till dark.
A rustling breeze shares secrets with flies,
And nature's laughter brings joyful sighs.

Crickets compose tunes in the twilight glow,
While snails take their time, enjoying the show.
A bustling ant starts a dance-off spree,
As the moon watches on, feeling carefree.

In this symphony silent yet loud,
Each creature's folly, a vibrant crowd.
Nature's comedy floats through the air,
In a world where laughter is everywhere.

Mementos of a Quiet Mind

A thought like a butterfly flits and flies,
Sometimes it lands where a cactus lies.
The mind wanders off on a leapfrog spree,
Chasing its tail like a curious puppy.

With every quiet tick of the clock's embrace,
Ideas erupt like a cake in your face.
The whispers of wisdom, all jumbled and neat,
Dance round the head - oh, a silly feat!

Memories linger like bubbles in air,
Popping with laughter, without a care.
Jokes from the past, like old friends, come round,
Reminding me giggles are often profound.

So here's to the quiet that brings forth the jest,
A playful retreat, where thoughts can rest.
In this gentle chaos, I find what I seek,
A chuckle or two makes the journey unique.

Garden of Echoes and Introspection

In the garden of musings, shadows grow tall,
A gnome cracks jokes, while the daisies all call.
Reflections of laughter dance on the ground,
As whispers of wisdom resound all around.

The roses conspire with the thorns they bear,
Planning their antics with a delicate flair.
Each petal a note in a symphonic tease,
Tickling the ears of the wandering breeze.

As caterpillars perform on a leaf,
They spin tales of folly, removing all grief.
The squirrels in suits, with top hats askew,
Giggle at antics, ever so new.

So here in this garden, where echoes do play,
The humor of stillness brightens the day.
With introspection, the heart finds its tune,
As laughter and wisdom dance under the moon.

The Alchemy of Whispered Hopes

In the cauldron of dreams, hopes bubble and brew,
A dash of a chuckle, a sprinkle of 'who knew?'
Mix potions of laughter with flavors of cheer,
And watch as the mundane becomes quite sincere.

The secret recipe stirs in the night,
With ingredients mixed in delight's pure light.
A pinch of the odd, a dollop of glee,
Turns woes into wonders, as fun as can be.

With whispers of fortune, the spirits arise,
Guiding the foolish, where laughter flies.
An elixir of joy, both silly and sweet,
Transforms hesitant hearts into rhythmic beats.

In the alchemy's grasp, life's troubles dissolve,
With giggles exploding, each puzzle evolves.
And all that remains is a grin on the face,
As hopes whisper softly, in a merry embrace.

Chronicles of the Inner Whisper

In the quiet, thoughts do chatter,
Like popcorn kernels, they bounce and scatter.
A tiny bug gets lost in the muse,
As I try to decide which pair of shoes.

Tickling my brain with playful jest,
The inner me sings, a curious guest.
Should I dance or should I snooze?
Oh, decisions, why do you confuse?

Musings from the Heart's Soil

A teapot spills secrets, steaming hot,
The biscuits crumble, oh, what a plot!
Shall I share a laugh or wear a frown?
With saucy jokes, I'll wear the crown.

My heart grows wild, like an untamed vine,
Twisting and tumbling, oh how I pine.
With a wink and a nudge, I'll take a leap,
Into the garden of thoughts, I safely creep.

Petals of Loneliness in Bloom

A lone rose giggles, dressed in pink,
While dandelions plot, in a thinking blink.
Why do they sway, feeling so grand?
In wind-borne whispers, they join a band!

Petals in a riddle, what do they say?
"Let's dance in the sun and giggle all day!"
Unless it rains, then we'll pout and sigh,
But secretly plan for a cheeky reply.

The Dialogue of Hidden Roots

Roots twist and turn beneath the earth,
Conspiring on matters of little worth.
"Who ate my lunch?" one root does exclaim,
"Was it you again, with your crafty game?"

The laughter erupts, underground they cheer,
Root pals uniting, sharing a beer.
With gnarled jokes and a knotty jest,
Life's a party, come join the fest!

Ponderings in the Wilderness

In the woods where thoughts run free,
I ponder if a squirrel can see.
Do trees get bored? They never talk,
Perhaps they gossip, just like a hawk.

A leaf flutters down like a feather,
Is it lost? Or just feeling clever?
The path twists around with a sneaky grin,
I chase my thoughts, where do I begin?

Caterpillars plotting their grand parade,
Why not a dance instead of a glade?
Moss takes its time in the sun's warm glow,
Is it lazy or just putting on a show?

The brook babbles tales of fishy flair,
Do they gossip of turtles that just don't care?
And as the clouds pillow fight in the sky,
I giggle at how they so aimlessly fly.

Chronicles of an Inner Voice

Jumbled thoughts march in a line,
Is today a good day to whine?
Echoes bounce, some stick like glue,
Why does my laughter sound like a shoe?

Imaginary debates with my stray sock,
Does it wish to join the clock?
Tick-tock, on tales of fluff and fate,
Oh dear! It lost a friend, what a state!

A sandwich replays its roll in bread,
Did the pickles ever feel misled?
While peanut butter just waits with a grin,
"Here comes the jelly, let the fun begin!"

The toilet hums a tune so shy,
Is it serenading the peel of a pie?
Each creak in the house holds a comic thought,
Am I the only one who's distraught?

Reflections in Still Waters

Ripples dance at the fish's joke,
Can frogs laugh? Or just croak and poke?
Mirror, mirror on the lake,
Is that my face? Or a pancake?

The lilies float, serene and sly,
Plotting their world beneath the sky.
"Let's wear a crown," one flower sings,
While a bee buzzes by with bouquets and flings.

A turtle swims with majestic grace,
Is he just trying to win a race?
"Slow and steady," he nudges a weed,
But talks no smack, just keeps up the speed.

The water laughs with every splash,
"Wouldn't it be fun to make a dash?"
And with each hop, a storyline flows,
Riddles of sunshine, the laughter grows.

Seeds of Contemplation

In a garden where dreams are pinned,
Daisies ruminate on where they've been.
One pops up with a curious stare,
"Do we talk to weeds? Is that debonair?"

A gnome listens in, quite surreal,
Is he a statue or just playing real?
With every chuckle, the daisies sway,
Plotting their schemes to rule the day.

The sun beams down like a spotlight bright,
Casting shadows that twist left and right.
A bug winks at me, oh what a sight,
"Do you think they know it's day or night?"

As I ponder with petals as my muse,
Life's little quirks amuse and confuse.
So here we are, in comedic plight,
Tending laughter in the warm twilight.

Echoing Silence: A Journey Within

In the attic of my mind, I roam,
Finding dust bunnies that seem like home.
They giggle and dance in the corners of thought,
All the while plotting, or so I've been taught.

A sock puppet speaks, 'You've got it all wrong!'
While my inner critic just hums a sad song.
The fridge door whispers, 'You're out of snacks!'
And I ponder if this is just one of my hacks.

I trip over dreams that are stacked in a row,
Hopes that have grown like weeds in a show.
A mirror just laughs, 'You've got quite the flair!'
'You dress like Picasso,' it says, 'in mid-air!'

As I exit the chaos, I tumble and slide,
Chasing my laughter, oh, what a wild ride!
Each echoing silence feels playful and bright,
In this journey within, I find pure delight.

When Whispers Take Root

In the garden of chatter, I sow what I can,
With a watering can filled with giggles and plans.
The daisies all nod as I share my good jokes,
While the beans in the back burst forth into folks.

The carrots just chuckle, 'We've seen better days!'
As the peas crack up over similar ways.
The sunflowers sway, draped in sun-kissed attire,
While the compost mutters, 'I'm deep in my mire.'

A rogue tomato sings of the woes of the vine,
'Love is all ketchup! Mustard's just fine!'
Roots intertwine in their humorous fight,
As laughter erupts in the fading daylight.

When whispers take root, you can't help but grin,
In the soil of my psyche, it's fun to begin.
So let's plant some stories and let them take flight,
In this garden of giggles, we'll dance through the night.

Fables from the Inner Garden

In a world of teacups where dreams blossom long,
I gather my fables and spin them in song.
The turtles tell tales of the races they lost,
While squirrels throw acorns just to make me toss.

A butterfly chuckles, 'I've seen it all here!'
Dancing through petals, spreading sunshine and cheer.
The toads in the pond sit grumpy and wise,
They croak out their wisdom without any guise.

Through whispers of nonsense, I wander and roam,
In the nooks of my garden, I've made a fine home.
Cabbages gossip, all dressed up in green,
Planting secrets of laughter, absurd and serene.

From these fables of joy, I learn to delight,
To break through the silence, make noise in the night.
In this inner garden, I flourish and play,
With characters charming, come brighten my day.

The Dance of Silent Whispers

The walls hum a tune only I can hear,
As shadows of secrets draw close, never fear.
A pair of old shoes start tapping away,
In moonlight, they giggle, inviting me play.

A clock with no hands bows down to the floor,
It means that I breathe with each tip-tapping score.
The giggles of echoes swirl 'round in my space,
Each silent whisper dons a peculiar face.

In waltz with my thoughts as they twirl in delight,
An ensemble of nonsense takes flight into night.
Arm in arm with the quiet, we jump and we spin,
In this dance of the silent, the joy does begin.

With such mirth around me, who needs to be loud?
In this theater of minds, we're the quirkiest crowd.
So come join the frolic, feel free to step near,
The dance of the whispers invites us to cheer!

The Anatomy of Inner Chatter

In the garden of my mind,
Thoughts take root, often unkind.
Weeds of doubt, sprouting fast,
Pulling me down, a chaotic blast.

I asked my brain for a plan,
It replied with a jumbled ran.
Procrastination blooms like dandelion,
With each excuse, I'm more reliant.

The voices laugh, they tease and play,
Gossiping on a sunny day.
I try to shoo them, but they stick,
Like bubblegum, just too thick.

Still, I giggle, losing the fight,
These inner chats turn day to night.
In this circus, I am the clown,
Juggling thoughts that tumble down.

Conversations with Shadows

I met my shadow in the hall,
It whispered secrets, gave me a call.
We share a joke about the light,
And dance with laughter through the night.

It claims to know my every move,
In the corner, it starts to groove.
Sometimes it trips me, just for fun,
Saying, "Come on, let's run, let's run!"

I argued with it, made a fuss,
"You're just a silhouette, not a plus!"
But it smirked back, with a sly grin,
"I catch your folly before it begins!"

Together we chuckle, oh what a sight,
Two oddballs, bantering with delight.
In this game of shadows, we both play,
Finding joy in the light of day.

Unraveling the Inner Monologue

In my head, thoughts whirl and spin,
A jigsaw puzzle with pieces thin.
I ponder deeply, but not too well,
Verbal chaos, it's quite the sell.

A self-help book I tried to read,
It said, "Be mindful," but I mislead.
I laughed so loud, I couldn't hear,
The wisdom lost, but jokes drew near.

I asked my brain for some wisdom, you see,
It replied, "Just eat more cake and tea!"
And thus, I found my revelation,
Sugar and giggles are my salvation.

As I unravel this mental knot,
Each thought that tangles, a funny plot.
A comedy in the mind's own lane,
Embracing folly, wisdom's inane.

Petals of Deliberation

In the garden of my daydreams bright,
Petals fall with each fleeting thought's flight.
I ponder this and I ponder that,
Like a thoughtful cat with a thinking hat.

What should I eat? Should I wear blue?
My inner voice laughs, "How about stew?"
With each decision, a chuckle and grin,
Life's a buffet—I'll take it all in!

I consult the flowers for advice, you see,
A daisy suggests, "Unique like me!"
But roses chime in, "Stick to the style,
Be thorny yet pretty, that works for a while."

So here I am in floral debate,
Wearing mismatched socks, oh what a fate!
With petals laughing, I guess I'll be fine,
In the garden of thoughts, I whimsically dine.

A Dance of Thoughts in the Breeze

Floating thoughts like dandelion fluff,
Got lost in the wind, can't find it tough.
Ideas twirl, in a whimsical spree,
Each one steps lightly, just to be free.

A giggle escapes from a wrinkle in time,
As musings hum softly, a nursery rhyme.
A ballet of minds in a topsy-turvy way,
Who knew that thought could dance and sway?

Twists and turns in this jovial flight,
Like socks in a dryer, a playful delight.
Chasing the clouds, laughing all the while,
Now I'm a thinker with a goofy smile!

The breeze carries whispers; oh what a game,
Thoughts acting silly, never the same.
As daydreams collide with the twilight's tease,
Who knew a ponder could shimmy with ease?

Elysium of Reflective Dreams

In the land of nod, where thoughts take a leap,
Chasing old socks while the world's asleep.
Mirrors of laughter reflect in my brain,
Wobbling thoughts like a rollercoaster train.

A parade of nonsense, all wearing a grin,
With cats on unicycles, such chaos within.
I ponder life's meaning on a swing set high,
While turtles in tutus are zooming on by.

Lollipops whisper in the stillness of night,
And dreams wear pajamas; oh, what a sight!
A festival of whimsy, light as a breeze,
Who knew reflections could bring such a tease?

Tickling my mind with their curious flair,
Thoughts prance around like they just don't care.
In this odd wonderland, where fun rules supreme,
I trip on my musings, a jolly mad dream!

The Muted Chorus of Contemplation

Whispers of whimsy curl in retreat,
A choir of chuckles, all light on their feet.
In the quiet of thought, a balloon pops loud,
And giggles erupt from the philosophy crowd.

Contemplation tries on a colorful hat,
While pondering whether to chase a fat cat.
Riddles play hopscotch in corners of gray,
As the muted chorus begins its odd play.

Underneath silent stars, ideas take flight,
Like balloon animals twirling in the night.
Each thought a note in this playful refrain,
Silly serenades dancing through my brain.

In the garden of whispers, ideas sprout wide,
As metaphors giggle while taking a ride.
It's a comedy show in the mind's quiet dome,
When thoughts start to sing, I feel right at home!

A Tapestry Woven in Silence

Threads of thought weave in a colorful dance,
Each one a giggle, a flicker, a chance.
In the loom of stillness, what strange knots appear,
Jokes told in shadows, a comedy sphere.

With laughter like threads, tangled in delight,
A tapestry brightens the velvety night.
Quilted in chuckles, a patchwork of cheer,
As musings prance lightly, making me leer.

Stitching together my curious dreams,
With a needle of whimsy that bursts at the seams.
Each seam a secret, every stitch a jest,
Creating a masterpiece of silliness blessed.

So here in this fabric of reflective mirth,
I find my own humor, a treasure of worth.
In the silence, the laughter unfurls and expands,
A woven creation by my giggling hands!

Voices of the Unheard

In the garden, whispers grow,
Tangled tales we never know.
Worms debate the weather gloom,
While crickets plot to steal the room.

Dandelions hold meetings late,
Arguing which flower's great.
The bees are buzzing loud for fun,
While snails race to see who's won.

Birds discuss their latest catch,
As squirrels play a game of hatch.
Underneath the leaves they meet,
With secret snacks and soft retreat.

So listen close, if you can bear,
In nature's choir, secrets share.
Among the weeds and flowers wild,
Lies laughter tossed, and laughter styled.

Dreams Planted in Silence

Quiet nights with stars aglow,
Dreams that tumble, slip, and flow.
A moonbeam sneezes, lightning bugs laugh,
While night's shadow plays the gaffe.

Turtles plot a night-time race,
With secret maps they try to trace.
The frogs cheer loud for their dear friend,
As whispers of ribbits softly blend.

Stars hold meetings in their flight,
Arguing which one's the most bright.
A comet zooms, it spills its tea,
While owls jest at its wild spree.

So dream your dreams in silent fun,
Where moonlit mischief's never done.
In darkness laughter finds its way,
Creating joy in night's ballet.

The Garden of Quiet Musings

In the stillness, thoughts take flight,
Among the blooms, ideas light.
A daisy daydreams of being grand,
While tulips plot to form a band.

Beetles boast of their fine skills,
In hushed tones, they share their thrills.
The pond reflects their tales of glee,
As frogs join in, a symphony.

Butterflies paint stories in the air,
While grasshoppers jump without a care.
In each corner, a giggle grows,
Sprouting laughter where nobody knows.

So stroll through dreams, both soft and sweet,
In the garden, where musings meet.
With every whisper, hearts take wing,
In this quiet place, joy's the king.

Hidden Dialogues of the Heart

In the shade where shadows dwell,
The heart hums its secret spell.
Petals murmur, softly sway,
As whispers dance in bright array.

A fox in disguise shares its tale,
Of morning runs and a funny fail.
While owls wink with knowing eyes,
Their hoots a song, a sweet surprise.

Allies of the night take charge,
As bright ideas take their large.
In tiny corners, laughter weaves,
Creating threads that no one leaves.

So listen close, within the dark,
For hidden dialogues leave a mark.
With every chuckle, life imparts,
The funny twists of hidden hearts.

Burgeoning Thoughts Under a Quiet Moon

In the still of night, ideas sprout,
Like mushrooms popping up, no doubt.
A squirrel in a hat, talking in rhyme,
Critiquing my dreams, wasting my time.

The moon winks at me, a cheeky friend,
As I debate if I should laugh or pretend.
Puns blooming like flowers, some quite absurd,
In this garden of nonsense, thoughts are unheard.

Dancing shadows chase a cat on the wall,
While I ponder if furniture has feelings at all.
A chair whispers secrets about its days,
While I ponder my extensive sock array.

Laughter echoes through this midnight spree,
As I question if socks conspire against me.
With every chuckle, I plant a new thought,
These midnight musings have tangled my plot.

Melodies of the Unsaid

In a world where words just trip and fall,
I sing to the plants; they might hear it all.
A cactus hums along, swaying to and fro,
While a daffodil giggles, putting on a show.

The silence plays music, a jumbled tune,
With squirrels as conductors beneath the moon.
They nod their heads, keeping time with their tails,
As I chase after thoughts that tease and derail.

Every unspoken word is a butterfly,
Flitting through the air with a wink and a sigh.
I tap my foot, trying to catch their flight,
As they giggle and scatter, oh, what a sight!

In this laughter of quiet, I find my place,
Dancing with shadows, a whimsical chase.
The melodies bloom in the lack of a song,
In the garden of silence, I finally belong.

Whispers of the Unspoken

In the pause between thoughts, a whisper may break,
An owlish insight, or perhaps a mistake.
A tumbleweed rolls by with a baffled gaze,
As I muse on the mysteries of socks and their ways.

They hold debates on who lost their mate,
Imagining dramas that linger till late.
With buttons as witnesses, they plot and they scheme,
Boxers and briefs giggle, a fabric-bound dream.

Philosophers argue in this fabric realm,
While I try to keep my thoughts at the helm.
A sock puppet clamors, 'Take life with some sass!'
"Why not?" I reply, "Let's skip on the grass!"

The unspoken whispers in a jumbled flight,
Bringing joy to the absurd in the still of the night.
As I lay down these thoughts with a chuckle and sigh,
I grasp the laughter that hides in the shy.

Flickers of Inner Dialogue

In the corners of my mind, ideas flicker,
Like fireflies dancing, lighting up quicker.
One suggests tacos, another wants cheese,
While my thoughts put on hats, just to tease.

A squirrel debates over pizza or pie,
As I wonder if rainbows drink soda to fly.
My inner voices are quite the grotesque,
Wrestling life choices in a comical mess.

A pair of mismatched socks conspire at dawn,
Plotting to hijack my shoes with a yawn.
As thoughts leap and bumble, a giggle erupts,
Reminding me daily, life's funny and clutched.

So I scribble these musings beneath the fun moon,
Where worries are jesters, and laughter's a boon.
With a wink to the stars, my thoughts take a bow,
In this flickering dance, I just laugh and allow.

Unraveled Threads of Thought

In my mind, a tangle grows,
Like yarn that's lost in little toes.
Cats pounce on every stray idea,
While socks conspire, disappear!

A jumbled mess of dreams in flight,
I question owls of day and night.
The fridge hums back, a judgmental sound,
As thoughts yarn-bomb the world around.

Caffeinated squirrels lead the dance,
While rubber ducks all take a chance.
Should I frolic in sunshine's glow,
Or just binge-watch a show from '90s, you know?

I'll pen a sonnet to the couch,
As my wisdom leaks like a friendly slouch.
Gladly lost in this chaotic spree,
Who knew thoughts could be so silly, not so free!

Soul-Cast Shadows on Earth

My shadow's got a mind of its own,
It dances and prances, always alone.
It mocks my style with a sway and a spin,
While I trip and tumble, it's laughing within.

We've had long chats about the moon,
Debating if it hums a funny tune.
It says, 'Why fear the light that I cast?'
As I chase it down streets, moving fast.

Lawn gnomes gossip about our strange plight,
They claim my shadow planned a social night.
In my dreams, I find it's running wild,
Filling the world with antics, so unbeguiled.

It draws silly faces, making me laugh,
While I'm stuck in lines, just doing the math.
Trust your shadow, it knows the way,
To a banquet of chuckles, in sun's warm play!

Conversations with the Invisible

I chat with ghosts that dance in my room,
They giggle and tease, like petals in bloom.
They tell me secrets wrapped in fine air,
While I sip my tea, oblivious to care.

Invisible friends read my mind's page,
They scribble in corners, acting their age.
Who knew that apparitions liked jokes?
Making puns from thin air, treating me like folks!

They argue about who's the best unseen,
Pretending to be a bustling machine.
I join their banter, apply for their team,
Finding joy in an imagination's gleam.

A thrill of laughter, lost in thin space,
With my ghostly pals, I keep up the pace.
So when you're alone, don't wear a frown,
Invite the unseen, let laughter abound!

Gossamer Threads of Solitude

In quiet corners, I weave my thoughts,
A spider crafting webs of what's sought.
Each strand's a giggle, a whimsy-filled fluke,
As I tickle the air, playing the kook.

I chase butterflies who refuse to stand still,
While ants negotiate snacks with great skill.
A sunflower grins, rooting for me,
While I clumsily juggle thoughts of lost glee.

How to make pie from clouds in the sky?
Pondering too long, and I'd rather just fly.
I whisk up the stars, blend laughter and light,
Turning solemn sighs into giggles, bright.

In this solitude, I dance with delight,
Over puddle mirrors reflecting the night.
For in quiet moments, the funny prevails,
Weaving gossamer threads, like true fairy tales!

Visions in a Quiet Frame

In the garden of my mind, I stroll,
Chasing thoughts that play the troll.
They giggle, dance, and steal my hat,
Oh look, there's a cat that thinks he's that!

A sunbeam sneaks to tickle my nose,
While laughter unravels where the wild thyme grows.
All the butterflies wear silly shoes,
And the daisies gossip with the evening hues.

Clouds float by with a cheeky smile,
They plot a prank every once in a while.
A whisper here, a chuckle there,
My own thoughts tease me with a dare.

As the moon peeks through the leafy greens,
I ponder the wacky sights that scene means.
In this noisy silence, joy remains,
With every thought, a set of chains.

The Heart's Unvoiced Journey

My heart's on a bus, it's quite absurd,
Taking routes I've never heard.
It honks at love, waves to despair,
While seatmates giggle, they just don't care!

Bumpy roads of unthought dreams,
In this ride, nothing's as it seems.
The driver winks at bygone fears,
As laughter peels away the years.

A squirrel's the navigator, bold and spry,
Pointing directions as clouds float by.
With every turn, I scratch my chin,
Perhaps the joy was the journey within!

At each stop, I gather more cheer,
Trading woes for giggles, that's the way here.
Oh, the heart's a traveler, light on its feet,
In this silent journey, it can't be beat!

Memoirs of Thought in Bloom

In the pot of ponder, I plant a thought,
Watered by dreams, it grows quite fraught.
A flower bursts forth, with petals of glee,
Waving its hands and shouting, 'Look at me!'

The winds bring whispers of silly schemes,
As clouds join in with whimsical beams.
Butterflies trip on their painted wings,
Chasing the rhythm that laughter brings.

Every thought's a bud, ready to bloom,
In the garden of giggles, there's always room.
Dancing bees share a jest or two,
Mimicking me, and that's nothing new!

As the sun sets down its golden crest,
With chortles echoing, I feel so blessed.
In this patch where chuckles are mixed,
My blooming thoughts have truly fixed!

The Collected Whispers of Reflection

In a quiet nook where echoes play,
Whispers flutter in a cheeky ballet.
They tickle the walls with secrets so sly,
Each giggle a breeze, each laugh the sky.

Reflections spin like tops on a whim,
Casting shadows that dance, not so dim.
Thoughts tie their shoes, ready to race,
In this game of mirth, there's plenty of space.

A wisp of a memory jumps in a fit,
Spreading stories of when I fell for a skit.
The mirror chuckles, can't keep it cool,
As I'm reminded of days spent at school.

When the night winds down, and laughter nears,
I sip on the echoes, drink in my cheers.
These collected whispers bring light to my heart,
In this joyous reflective, I have my part!

The Quiet Movement of Thought

In a corner of my brain, thoughts play hide and seek,
They giggle like children, but they're far from meek.
They dance a little jig, then they trip on a shoe,
And whisper to each other, "What shall we do?"

A whirl of ideas that twirl and spin round,
Like squirrels on espresso, they bounce with a sound.
Some ideas are puns, others puns gone wrong,
In the quiet of thinking, I'm writing a song.

While pondering in silence, I'm caught in a snare,
Like a cat with a laser, I'm dreaming of air.
Each notion is playful, like puppies at play,
But my focus is fickle—time slips away!

In this cerebral circus, my thoughts are the show,
They tumble and juggle; oh, where did they go?
But laughter erupts from the chaos inside,
For in the funny business, my worries do hide.

Brooding in the Greenhouse of the Mind

In a garden of fancies, my brain starts to sprout,
Thoughts mixing like salad, a curious clout.
I water them softly with giggles and sighs,
And watch as they blossom, oh, what a surprise!

Though some thoughts are weeds, they pop up with glee,
"I'm deep-rooted in nonsense! Come garden with me!"
And as I tend to them, I can't help but grin,
For the funniest flowers grow thicker within.

Pondering the petals, absurd and absurdest,
Like roses in tutu's, my mind's at its weirdest.
Each bloom is a quirk, a jester in play,
In the greenhouse of laughter, they dance all day.

As I prune and I shape them, they twist and they tease,
I wonder, can I plant some thoughts with more ease?
But with every new sprout, I'm lost in the plot,
In this quirky garden, who knows what I've got?

The Hidden Orchard of Reflection

In the orchard of memory, I wander and roam,
Picking thoughts like apples, I'm carving my tome.
Some are juicy and sweet, while others are tart,
But each one's a giggle that tickles the heart.

I've stumbled on treasures, I chuckle and muse,
Like a squirrel with a stash, I can't help but choose.
A basket of quirks, oh, I'll take them all,
In this hidden orchard, I'm having a ball!

The branches are shaking with laughter galore,
As I pluck silly notions from life's whimsical store.
With reflections so funny, my mind starts to gleam,
In this orchard of wonder, I'm living a dream.

So here I shall linger, beneath these odd trees,
Gathering chuckles like leaves in the breeze.
And as the sun sets on this merry expedition,
I'll savor each thought, ripe with tradition.

Seeds of Reflection

In the soil of my mind, thoughts are scattered and spry,
Like popcorn in a theater, they jump and they fly.
Each kernel a giggle, a thought wrapped in jest,
I'm planting these memories, letting them rest.

With laughter as sunshine, they bloom into glee,
Every chuckle a bloom, wild and carefree.
Some thoughts grow like vines, tangled and silly,
While others burst forth with a bright, happy willy.

The garden is raucous, a comedic parade,
With crooning cucumbers and jokes that won't fade.
The more that I ponder, the funnier it gets,
In this patch of reflection, I'm free of regrets.

So I'll water these thoughts with the humor I find,
In the fertile landscape of my quirky mind.
For each silly seed that I plant with delight,
Grows laughter eternal, a joyful insight.

The Stillness of Emerging Thoughts

In the quiet of my mind's retreat,
Thoughts bounce around, oh what a feat!
Like squirrels on a daring spree,
Searching for acorns they just can't see.

Whispers of brilliance mingle with doubt,
Like a dog barking but too far out.
I chuckle at worries that won't take flight,
While munching on cookies, it feels so right.

A parade of ideas with silly hats,
Marching to rhythms of chatting cats.
I'll scribble them down, short and sweet,
Like candy for thoughts—oh, can't be beat!

Before the day fades, let's make a plan,
To dance with our dreams like no one can.
In the stillness, I'll find my muse,
And laugh at the thoughts that I might refuse.

Parables from the Inner Realm

A tale unfolds from within my head,
Where turtles wear sneakers, and snails just dread.
They debate the best routes to take each week,
Over tea made from leaves that birds might speak.

What wisdom lies in a crinkled page,
Each scribble a dance, a thoughtful stage?
I can see the owls nodding, wise and sly,
As I offer my prayers to the passing fly.

With giggles and quirks, my mind takes flight,
On paper airplanes in the dim twilight.
I'll pen down the laughter, the glances of glee,
And ponder if ants can really be free.

Parables sprout like flowers in May,
Teaching me lessons in the goofiest way.
A chuckle, a sigh, on this journey I roam,
In my mind's funny land, I feel right at home.

Nuances of a Thoughtful Heart

Within me dwells a heart that sings,
With thoughts that flutter like butterfly wings.
It skips through fields of eccentric dreams,
Chasing after the oddest of schemes.

A careful dance of joy and jest,
As my pensive heart takes a comedic rest.
Each nuance wrapped in a chuckling sigh,
Winking at clouds that float by.

With a grin, it analyzes the world so wide,
Playing hopscotch down this merry ride.
Oh, the folly of matters so grand,
Is lost in the fun we misplace in the sand.

The heart's a joker, dressed up for fun,
Playing tricks till the rising sun.
In the nuances of laughter, I find my part,
As I dance with the whims of a thoughtful heart.

The Poetry of Finding Oneself

In the mirror, I meet a stranger's grin,
Am I wiser or just full of whim?
With crumbs on my shirt from snacks I devour,
I ponder my purpose at half past the hour.

A map of my life with doodles and marks,
Guides me through parks and playful barks.
Each twist and turn, a giggling adventure,
Finding myself in a wild, odd censure.

My thoughts scribble verses, a little offbeat,
Like dancing penguins in search of a seat.
In the rhythm of chaos, I trip not in fear,
But leap like a frog, full of cheer.

The poetry flows as I wander and weave,
In the fabric of laughter, I dare to believe.
As I tiptoe through life, a jester's delight,
Finding myself in the humor of night.

Whispers Entwined in Thought

In the garden of my brain, they sprout,
Little ideas wiggle about.
One says, "I'm a veggie, can't you see?"
The other retorts, "No, I'm a pea!"

In the chatter, a pickle gets loud,
Proclaiming proudly, "I'm in a crowd!"
But no one can hear this chatterbox,
For I'm too busy counting my socks.

Out pops a thought like a rubber band,
"What if unicorns start a band?"
They'd miss the mark, just dancing away,
While I laugh till my thoughts fade to gray.

Hilarious notions all come to play,
As I scratch my head and drift away.
With each grin, my brain does a flip,
Let's gather these thoughts, they're ripe for a trip!

The Reveal of Hidden Perspectives

Behind the curtain, ideas collide,
One thought tiptoes, then takes a slide.
"What if cats plan to run the show?"
The dog rolls his eyes and starts to growl slow.

A squirrel hops in, dressed like a king,
Holding a scepter, declaring a fling.
"In my kingdom, nuts reign supreme!"
While my coffee spills, disrupting the dream.

Each twist reveals a quirky display,
How the clouds laugh at the sun's bright ray.
With perspectives shifting like socks in the dryer,
I ponder aloud and the thoughts grow higher.

At last, I conclude with a silly grin,
Life's a circus, let the fun begin!
Each script unfolds like a joke on repeat,
In this comedy club, we take a front seat.

Cascading Thoughts in Serene Spaces

Thoughts tumble down like a waterfall's dance,
Tripping over each like a clown's lost prance.
A whimsical notion takes flight in the breeze,
"Do fish wear socks? Would that bring them ease?"

The moon chuckles softly, a cosmic delight,
As stars pop popcorn, twinkling bright.
"Hey, do you see that? The Milky Way's glow!"
"Yeah! But where do pizza toppings go?"

In this serene spot, my mind's in a whirl,
Where do bananas go when they twirl?
Laughter echoes in the bubbles of thought,
A carnival ride with joy that's sought.

So here I sit, tangled in dreams,
Plotting a story that blinks and beams.
Each thought a balloon floating up in the sky,
Where laughter and whimsy are never shy.

Hush of the Soul

In a quiet nook where thoughts like to play,
A whisper once told me, "Try saying 'Hey!'"
But I laughed so hard, it turned into snorts,
And suddenly, I was in funny retorts.

"Would a potato wear shoes if it could?"
And I pondered in silence, that's pretty good.
How sprightly the veggies would march down the lane,
In a fruit-and-veg festival, oh what a gain!

A chicken sidles up, pecking my dreams,
Saying, "Let's plan the world's biggest ice cream!"
The cows moo in sync, sharing a laugh,
As I jot down my plans on a little graph.

Inside this hush, giggles and quirks thrive,
As thoughts dance around, feeling so alive.
In my cozy mind, humor takes its toll,
As I savor the echoes, the hush of my soul.

The Symphony of a Thoughtful Heart

A thought danced lightly, one sunny day,
It slipped on a banana peel, quite the display.
It hummed a tune, offbeat and bold,
As whispers of giggles around it unfolded.

With twirls and spins, a comedy arose,
A heart that pondered in purple prose.
Each chuckle echoed as clouds rolled in,
A symphony struck with laughter to win.

The stars giggled shyly behind wooly confines,
As thoughts formed like jello in whimsical lines.
A tickle of joy, a pinch of surprise,
The ballet of musings brought tears to our eyes.

So let every heartbeat sing out with cheer,
And make a crescendo for all to hear.
In the merry cacophony of clever delight,
Our thoughtful hearts dance, oh what a sight!

Reflection's Sown Moments

In a mirror's glance, a wink and a grin,
A fly on the wall joined in with a spin.
Reflecting on dreams with a head full of fluff,
I laughed at my socks, mismatched and tough.

I pondered my choices, a riddle unplanned,
While grapes held a meeting on yielding their brand.
Each grape had a joke that fell flat on the floor,
Just like my attempts at a grand metaphor.

The clock ticked on, with its humorous chime,
Counting my thoughts in their playful prime.
With every tick-tock, a giggle grew loud,
As wishes and wishes formed a merry crowd.

So remember to chuckle while you self-reflect,
In silliness found, life's moments collect.
A mirror may show, just a face and a peep,
But it holds all the laughter we oftentimes keep.

Cultivating Solitude: An Inner Harvest

In my garden of thoughts, I plant with great care,
A wish for a radish that's got more flair.
Oh, the carrots are growing, but they wiggle with pride,
While cabbage just sits there, tongue-in-cheek, wide.

Sunflowers gossip, their heads held up high,
They share the latest buzz about clouds passing by.
And in this great silence, I chuckle and grin,
At the zinnias plotting a colorful win.

Beneath all the gossip and banter in green,
A leaf may just laugh at the world that's unseen.
With each sprout that rises, mirth fills the air,
As laughter blooms brightly, a joy that we share.

So tend to this garden with humor and light,
For solitude's harvest is pure delight.
In laughter, we nourish the seeds of our soul,
With each tasty giggle, we feel more whole.

Spaces of Silent Reckoning

In corners of quiet, where thoughts like to play,
A squirrel in a beret takes life day by day.
He scribbles profound notes in acorn-laden dreams,
In a space full of silence, or so it seems.

With solemn expressions, the shadows unfold,
As echoes of giggles, their secrets they hold.
The walls seem to whisper, perhaps they can see,
A laughter that bubbles from pondering me.

A solemn faced teapot high up on a shelf,
Ponders its purpose, or is it itself?
With each brewing thought that gently steams high,
I chuckle at musings that flutter and fly.

So embrace the stillness, where laughter has found,
A harmony lurking, just waiting around.
In the spaces of silence, let joy take its turn,
For even a moment is yours to discern.

Fragrant Echoes of Solitude

In a garden where silence blooms,
The daisies gossip, share their looms.
A squirrel debates with a lazy bee,
While pondering the fate of an old tree.

But what's that scent wafting near?
It's not grass, it's the thoughts, I fear!
Oh, my mind plays tricks like a jester,
Dancing with shadows, a wild investor.

The daisies chuckle, a comical sight,
As visions take flight, both day and night.
A cacophony of giggles, swirling around,
In the quietest place, humor is found.

So here in the stillness, laughter prevails,
While thoughts tumble like playful snails.
An orchestra of silliness starts to play,
In the fragrant echoes of a lonely day.

Labors of Contemplative Growth

I ponder my roots while sipping tea,
Wondering if the world can see me.
A flower's dilemma, what's it all for?
To stand tall or hide, that's the core!

In this field of musings, I trip and fall,
While daisies conspire, they rally and call.
With every thought, my branches spread wide,
Yet here comes a weed, on a joyride!

I planted a smile, watered with glee,
But weeds kept popping, oh, woe is me!
Thus, the laughter grows like wild vines,
Chasing my worries with whimsical lines.

So let's celebrate flaws in this patch,
With jokes and jests, I'll make a good match.
As I toil with wisdom, my heart takes a bow,
In contemplative growth, I say "Wow!"

Itineraries of an Unseen Mind

With maps of thoughts, I roam the skies,
Where giggles abound and humor flies.
An unseen mind, oh the places it goes,
In corners of laughter, curiosity grows.

I chart my routes on a narrow line,
Through fields of whimsy, the sun will shine.
But beware: detours lead to a chuckle,
Where logic stumbles, dreams start to buckle.

I boarded a thought train bound for fun,
Past fields of puns, oh it's all been spun.
The conductor whistles, "Next stop, delight!"
Onward we go, hearts feeling light.

So join my journey, let giggles entwine,
In this comical trek, we'll sip on sunshine.
With itineraries of mischief in tow,
The unseen mind is a marvelous show!

Reflections on Woven Benches

On a woven bench where odd thoughts sit,
I scribble down nonsense, bit by bit.
A squirrel reads poetry, a bird writes reviews,
While I sip my coffee and ponder my views.

The laughter of daisies softly unfolds,
As stories of shade and sunlight are told.
Oh, what a scene! It's hilarity bound,
In this tapestry of giggles, joy is found.

Reflections ripple like ponds of delight,
Where silliness dances from morning to night.
In this garden of musings, all's fair game,
Where absurdity thrives and laughter's the aim.

So come take a seat, adult or a lad,
On these woven benches, abandon the sad.
In reflections of comedy, let's all rejoice,
For in every giggle, we find our voice!

Whispers of the Silent Grove

In a grove where whispers play,
Trees gossip all night and day.
A squirrel chuckles at a crow,
"You're late for your audition, you know!"

The flowers nod their heads in glee,
While ants debate on who's the bee.
A snail holds court on a mossy throne,
While toads croak out their comical tone.

The wind brings tales of a clumsy hare,
Who tried to dance but slipped in a lair.
The leaves rustle with laughter shared,
As even the bushes seem quite prepared.

So in this grove, we find our jest,
Nature's humor is truly the best.
"Shhh," whispers the breeze, "you'll wake the sun,"
But even the dawn chuckles, "Oh, this is fun!"

Echoes of an Unspoken Dream

In dreams where nonsense takes its flight,
A chicken stood tall, claimed it could write.
"See my memoirs of life on the farm,"
While cows rolled their eyes, wide-eyed and warm.

A fish in a bowl rehearses a play,
"Me? An actor? Oh, what a day!"
The audience, a cat with a snooze,
Reads the script of a leaky old ruse.

A worm in the ground shares jokes with the bees,
While clouds giggle softly, swaying like trees.
A parrot chimes in, "Do it again!"
As applause erupts from the critters' den.

So echo through dreams, let laughter resound,
In this wacky world, joy can be found.
The absurdity dances on soft, gentle air,
With each quirky tale, let's all be aware.

The Language of Sown Thoughts

A carrot dreams of being a star,
While peas plot their path from afar.
"Break a leg," yells the leafy green,
As radishes giggle, unseen and serene.

Tomatoes flash their red, bold hues,
Claiming to toss the best of reviews.
The lettuce pretends to have high class,
While cucumbers roll, good humor to amass.

"Who's the funniest in our garden scene?"
As pots of herbs laugh, so keen and green.
Chives shout, "I'm sharp, I deserve the crown!"
And thus the gossip spreads all around.

So linger in thoughts where laughter sows,
In this playful patch, joy surely grows.
The whispers of veggies, quite low-key,
Unravel the secrets of glee's esprit.

Reflections Beneath the Surface

Beneath the pond where chuckles rise,
Frogs throw banter, oh so wise.
A fish swished by, snorted with grace,
"I'm the speedster in this watery race!"

The turtles debate who's fastest to flee,
While dragonflies swagger, just wait and see.
"Look at me!" says one with a flair,
Performing loops in midair, quite rare.

Ripples giggle at the silly scene,
As every onlooker can clearly glean.
Who says the deep needs to be so grave?
In this waterscape, humor we save.

So splash about, let laughter unfurl,
Under the surface, a joyful whirl.
Reflections dance, with every new wave,
In this world of whimsy, we all misbehave.

Veils of Thought in the Morning Mist

Foggy thoughts dance in my head,
Like lost socks under the bed.
I sip my coffee, miss the mug,
It's a comedy, a gentle shrug.

Gremlins steal my plans for the day,
They laugh and twist the words I say.
I chase reflections in the dew,
But all they do is laugh and skew.

Puns float around, take a quick bow,
Jokes in the ether, I wonder how?
I joke with birds, they chirp in glee,
Their wisdom tickles, it's just for me.

Laughter echoes through the trees,
Breezes carry it with ease.
In morning's light, absurdity reigns,
I embrace the quirk, forget the chains.

Unspoken Tales from the Depths

In the deep, shadows play games,
Whispers of fish with silly names.
Octopus winks, a Kraken pranks,
Bubbles pop like whispered thanks.

Jellyfish float with grace and flair,
Telling secrets without a care.
Shells crack jokes, laugh like a clown,
While seaweed sways, giggles abound.

Anemones dance in silent cheer,
Their antics tickle, we can't help but leer.
Starfish plan their next big jest,
Life's a splash, never a rest.

In depths of blue, laughter's the rule,
Underwater fun, who needs a school?
With fins and flippers, we dive and play,
Each bubble carries joy away.

The Stillness That Speaks

In a room where silence sings,
Dust bunnies wear imaginary things.
A clock ticks slow, like a sleepy rhyme,
Time finds humor in the mundane climb.

A chair creaks softly, shares its tale,
Of picnics gone wrong and ice cream fails.
Cushions giggle, they tell no lies,
As the cat snoozes and dreams of pies.

Windows peep with sunlight's grin,
And curtains sway like a dance within.
The stillness hums, it lightly pokes,
Reminding us of the joy in jokes.

So here in stillness, we find the beat,
Laughter lingers, it can't be beat.
In quiet moments, humor grows,
With every tick, the spirit knows.

Shadows of Yearning Under Starlight

Beneath the stars, my dreams commute,
But my wishes dance in a silly suit.
The moon snickers, a bright balloon,
While fireflies wink, a cheeky tune.

Whispers float on the midnight breeze,
Unruly shadows play with ease.
A longing glance from a friendly cat,
With paws of mischief, how about that?

I yearn for laughter, wild and free,
As crickets chirp a symphony.
The night wraps me in giggling dreams,
Where nothing's quite as funny as it seems.

In starlit whispers, joy takes flight,
Beneath the cosmos, everything's bright.
I let the comedy unfold each night,
In shadows of yearning, a whimsical sight.

www.ingramcontent.com/pod-product-compliance
Lightning Source LLC
Chambersburg PA
CBHW051632160426
43209CB00004B/618